Jr. Graphic Environmental Dangers™

Sinister Sludge

Oil Spills and the Environment

I0806647

Daniel R. Faust

PowerKiDS press
New York

Published in 2009 by The Rosen Publishing Group, Inc.
29 East 21st Street, New York, NY 10010

Copyright © 2009 by The Rosen Publishing Group, Inc.

All rights reserved. No part of this book may be reproduced in any form without permission in writing from the publisher, except by a reviewer.

First Edition

Editors: Joanne Randolph
Book Design: Greg Tucker
Illustrations: Dheeraj Verma/Edge Entertainment

Library of Congress Cataloging-in-Publication Data

Faust, Daniel R.
Sinister sludge : oil spills and the environment / Daniel R. Faust. — 1st ed.
p. cm. — (Jr. graphic environmental dangers)
Includes bibliographical references and index.
ISBN 978-1-4042-4230-2 (library binding) — ISBN 978-1-4042-4597-6 (pbk.) —
ISBN 978-1-4042-3982-1 (6-pack)
1. Oil spills—Environmental aspects—Juvenile literature. I. Title.
TD196.P4F38 2009
363.738'2—dc22
2007049699

Manufactured in the United States of America
CPSIA Compliance Information: Batch #WR218170RC: For further Information contact Rosen Publishing, New York, New York at 1-800-237-9932.

Contents

Introduction

Did you know that each of us uses products made from oil, called petroleum products, every day? We use them to help us do many things, such as heating our homes and fueling our cars. Petroleum products certainly make life easier for us. Finding, producing, moving, and using petroleum must not cause any problems, right? Wrong!

Oil spills from ships, drilling, and underwater pipelines can really hurt the **environment**. How can we keep this sinister, yet useful, sludge from harming our planet? Read on and find out!

SINISTER SLUDGE
OIL SPILLS AND THE ENVIRONMENT
A GROUP OF VOLUNTEERS LED BY MR. CLAUSEN ARE ON THEIR WAY TO THE DELAWARE RIVER TO STUDY THE TERRIBLE EFFECTS OF AN OIL SPILL ON THE ENVIRONMENT.
THE VOLUNTEERS ARE ALSO GOING TO HELP CLEAN UP THE SPILL AND RESCUE THE WILDLIFE AFFECTED.

MR. CLAUSEN'S WIFE, DR. ELLEN CLAUSEN, IS A SCIENTIST WHO WORKS FOR THE ENVIRONMENTAL PROTECTION AGENCY (EPA)*.
ALRIGHT, EVERYONE. LET'S GET STARTED.
AS WE HEAD OVER TO PICK UP THE GEAR WE'LL NEED, DR. CLAUSEN CAN PROVIDE SOME BACKGROUND ON THIS SPILL AND WHAT IT WILL MEAN FOR THE ENVIRONMENT.
MR. CLAUSEN AND THE OTHER VOLUNTEERS HOPE TO GET FIRSTHAND EXPERIENCE OF THE LASTING **DAMAGE** OIL SPILLS CAN DO. THEY ALSO HOPE TO GAIN SOME INSIGHT ON HOW TO KEEP THE ENVIRONMENT SAFE SO THEY CAN SPREAD THE WORD TO OTHERS.
*THE EPA IS AN AGENCY OF THE UNITED STATES CHARGED WITH PROTECTING HUMAN HEALTH AND SAFEGUARDING THE ENVIRONMENT.

"THE DELAWARE RIVER IS AN IMPORTANT WATERWAY FOR THE EASTERN PART OF THE UNITED STATES.
"SHIPS CAN USE THE RIVER TO TRAVEL BETWEEN MARYLAND, PENNSYLVANIA, NEW JERSEY, AND NEW YORK.
"BUT, LIKE CARS ON A BUSY HIGHWAY, SOMETIMES THESE SHIPS CAN HAVE ACCIDENTS.

"ON THE NIGHT OF NOVEMBER 26, THE ATHOS 1, AN OIL TANKER, WAS DAMAGED AND BEGAN SPILLING OIL INTO THE DELAWARE RIVER.
"ABOUT 30,000 GALLONS (113,562 L) OF CRUDE OIL, OR PETROLEUM, SPILLED INTO THE RIVER."*
*CRUDE OIL, OR PETROLEUM, IS THE TERM USED FOR OIL THAT HAS JUST BEEN REMOVED FROM THE EARTH AND MAY STILL HAVE UNWANTED MATTER IN IT.

WE ARE ALL HERE TODAY BECAUSE OF PETROLEUM.
BUT I BET MOST OF YOU USE PETROLEUM PRODUCTS EVERY DAY. A FEW OF YOU MIGHT BE SURPRISED AT SOME OF THE THINGS WE USE OIL FOR.

"PETROLEUM IS USED TO MAKE GASOLINE, WHICH IS USED AS FUEL FOR CARS.
"BUT, IT IS ALSO USED TO HEAT OUR HOMES IN THE WINTER,
"TO MAKE THINGS LIKE PLASTIC AND CRAYONS,
"AND TO MAKE WAX FOR CANDLES."

WHERE DOES PETROLEUM COME FROM, DR. CLAUSEN?
PETROLEUM IS MADE FROM PLANTS AND ANIMALS THAT DIED A LONG TIME AGO.

"A LOT OF PLANTS AND ANIMALS LIVE NEAR WATER.
"WHEN THEY DIE, MANY PLANTS AND ANIMALS FALL TO THE BOTTOM OF THE WATER.

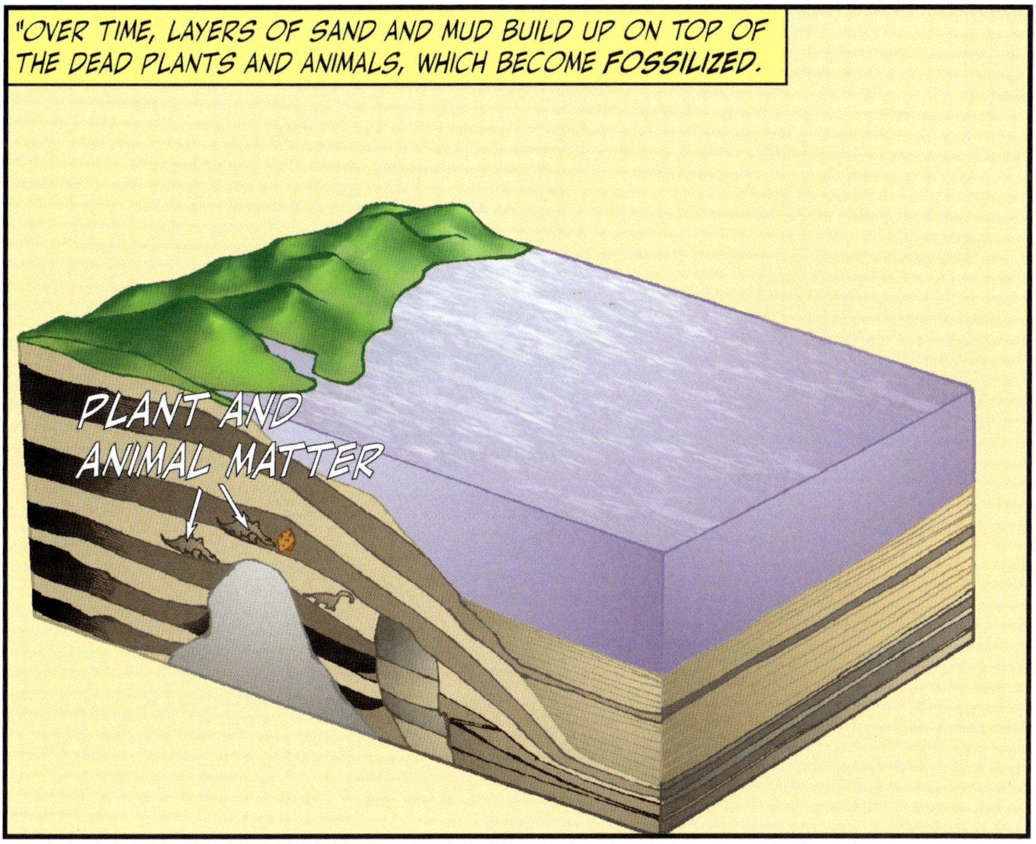
"OVER TIME, LAYERS OF SAND AND MUD BUILD UP ON TOP OF THE DEAD PLANTS AND ANIMALS, WHICH BECOME **FOSSILIZED**.
PLANT AND ANIMAL MATTER

"ALL THE LAYERS OF SAND AND MUD PRESS DOWN ON THE LOWER LAYERS. THE PRESSURE AND HEAT CREATED TURNS THE DEAD PLANTS AND ANIMALS INTO OIL.
OIL
"THAT IS WHY OIL IS SOMETIMES CALLED A FOSSIL FUEL.

"OIL IS FOUND DEEP UNDER GROUND.
"PUMPS AND **DERRICKS** ARE BUILT ON LAND WHERE OIL HAS BEEN FOUND.

"WHEN OIL IS DISCOVERED BENEATH THE OCEAN, OFFSHORE DRILLING PLATFORMS ARE BUILT.
"THE OIL CAN EITHER BE SENT DIRECTLY TO THE MAINLAND THROUGH A PIPELINE OR LOADED ONTO A TANKER.

"SINCE OIL CAN BE FOUND ONLY IN CERTAIN PLACES ON EARTH, MANY COUNTRIES HAVE THE OIL THEY NEED SHIPPED TO THEM IN LARGE SHIPS CALLED TANKERS.
"THESE SHIPS CAN CARRY MANY BILLIONS OF GALLONS (L) OF CRUDE OIL."

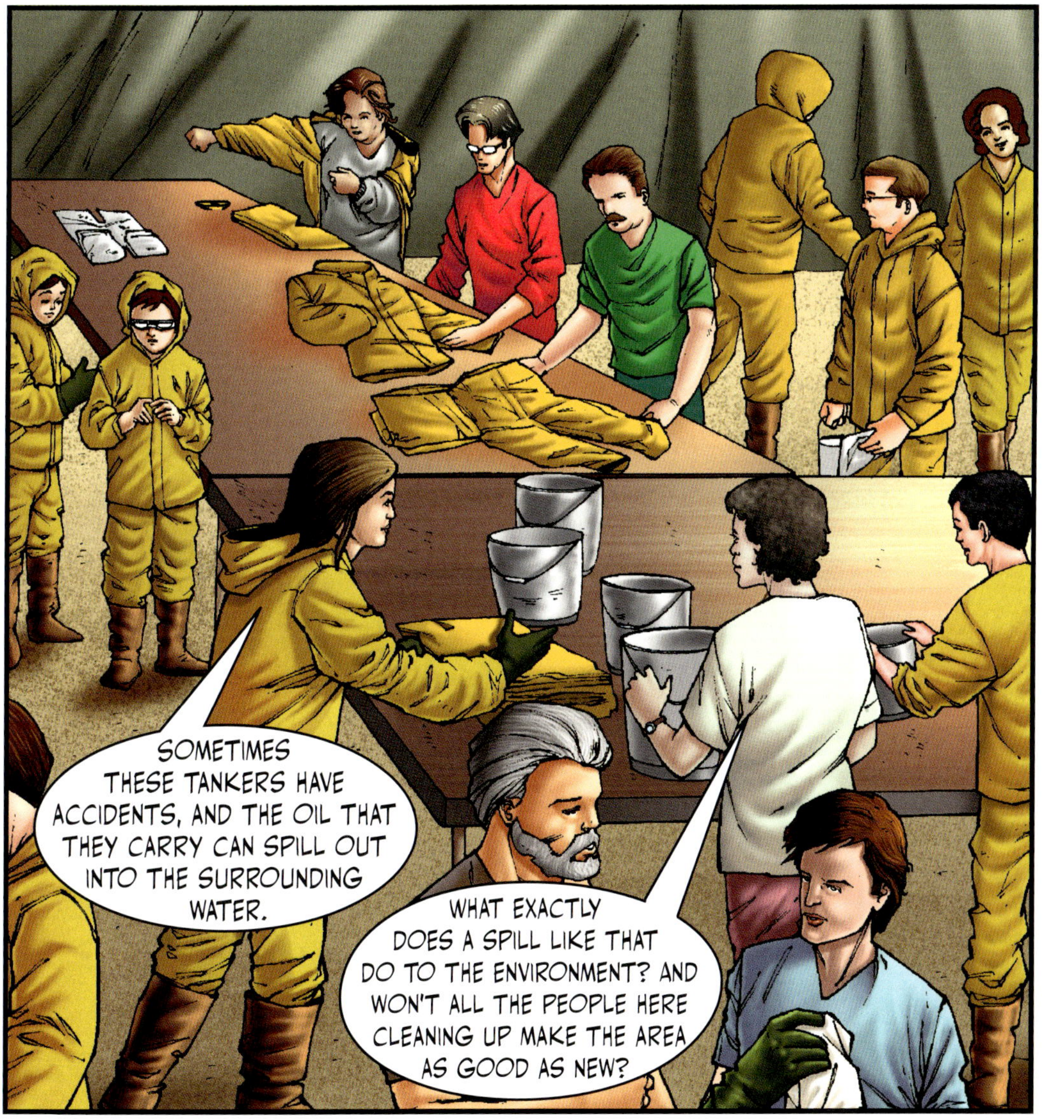
SOMETIMES THESE TANKERS HAVE ACCIDENTS, AND THE OIL THAT THEY CARRY CAN SPILL OUT INTO THE SURROUNDING WATER.
WHAT EXACTLY DOES A SPILL LIKE THAT DO TO THE ENVIRONMENT? AND WON'T ALL THE PEOPLE HERE CLEANING UP MAKE THE AREA AS GOOD AS NEW?

UNFORTUNATELY, NO. EVEN AFTER ALL THE WORK WE DO, THE IMPACT ON THE ENVIRONMENT WILL LIKELY BE FELT FOR UP TO 30 YEARS.
SOME PLANTS AND ANIMALS MAY NEVER RECOVER. LET ME BREAK IT DOWN FOR YOU.

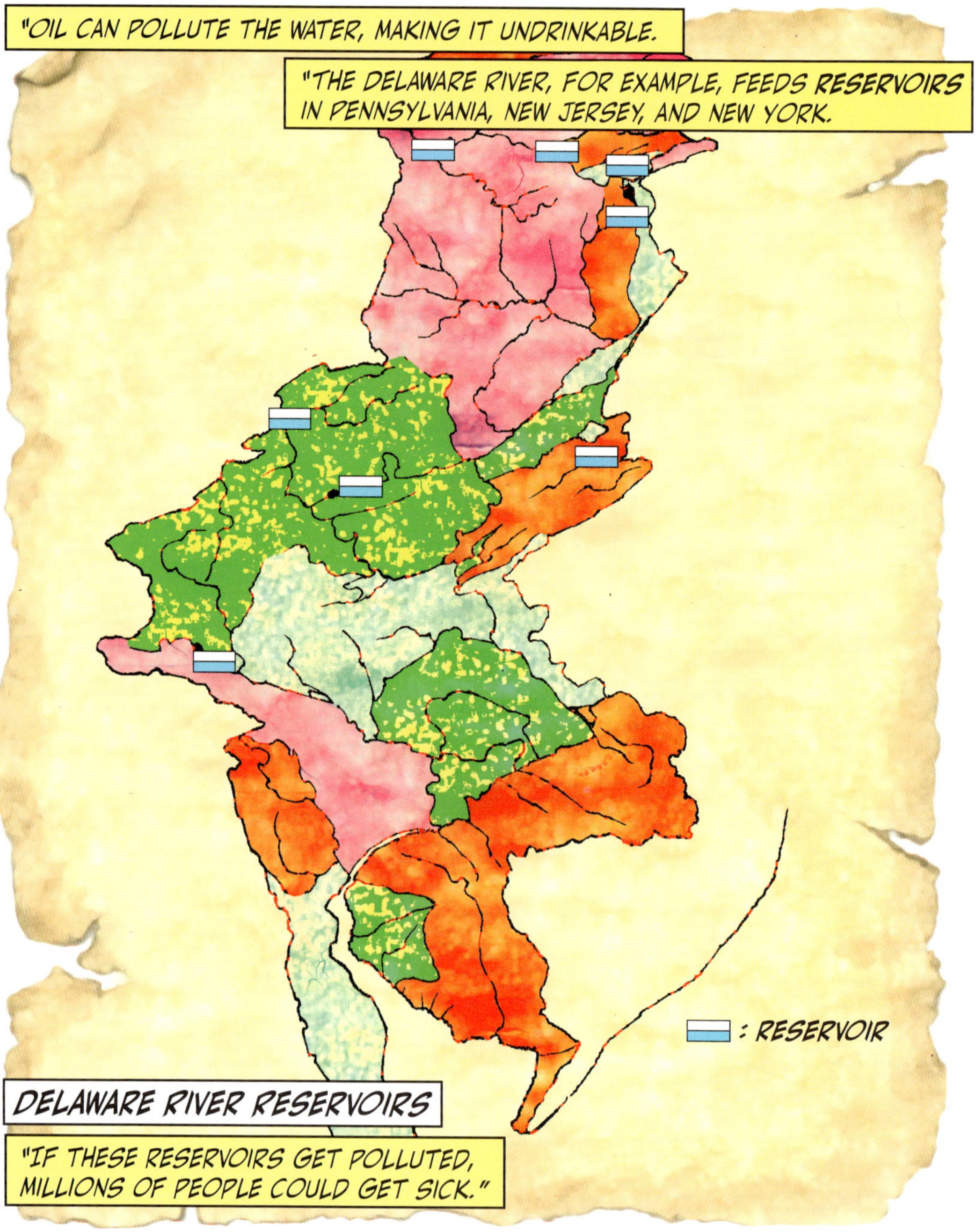
"OIL CAN POLLUTE THE WATER, MAKING IT UNDRINKABLE.
"THE DELAWARE RIVER, FOR EXAMPLE, FEEDS RESERVOIRS IN PENNSYLVANIA, NEW JERSEY, AND NEW YORK.
: RESERVOIR
DELAWARE RIVER RESERVOIRS
"IF THESE RESERVOIRS GET POLLUTED, MILLIONS OF PEOPLE COULD GET SICK."

AS YOU CAN SEE FROM LOOKING AT THIS POOR GUY, OIL IS ALSO TOXIC FOR BIRDS, FISH, AND ANIMALS.
AND THE SAD FACT IS THAT DESPITE OUR RESCUE EFFORTS, MOST OF THESE ANIMALS WILL PROBABLY NOT LIVE.

"AN ANIMAL CAN GET SICK IF IT SWALLOWS OIL OR BREATHES IN OIL'S TOXIC FUMES.
"IF OIL COVERS AN ANIMAL'S FUR OR FEATHERS, IT PREVENTS THE ANIMAL FROM KEEPING ITSELF WARM.

"IF ENOUGH FISH IN AN AREA DIE, IT CAN AFFECT THE FISHING BUSINESS IN THAT AREA.
"NOT ONLY DOES THAT MEAN NO FISH FOR DINNER, BUT IT ALSO MEANS THAT THE MEN AND WOMEN WHO EARN A LIVING FROM FISHING ARE OUT OF WORK."

THAT'S WHY PEOPLE HAVE TO REACT QUICKLY TO CLEAN UP AN OIL SPILL IF ONE HAPPENS.
THE OIL NEEDS TO BE CONTAINED BEFORE IT CAN DO TOO MUCH DAMAGE.
THESE WORKERS HERE ARE WORKING TO SKIM OIL THAT HAS MADE IT PAST THE BOOM.

WHAT'S A BOOM? IS THAT HOW WE CLEAN UP A SPILL?

"THERE ARE SEVERAL WAYS, MICHAEL.
"ONE WAY IS TO SKIM THE OIL OUT OF THE WATER.
"OIL CONTAINMENT BOOMS ARE USED TO CORRAL THE OIL, WHICH IS THEN COLLECTED WITH SKIMMERS. BUT, THIS NEEDS TO BE DONE BEFORE THE OIL HAS TIME TO SPREAD.

"SPILT OIL CAN ALSO BE BURNED, TURNING THE OIL INTO A GAS, WHICH GETS **DISPERSED** INTO THE ATMOSPHERE.
"OF COURSE, BURNING TOO MUCH OIL IN ONE PLACE COULD CAUSE JUST AS MUCH DAMAGE TO THE SURROUNDING ENVIRONMENT AS THE SPILL ITSELF.

"CHEMICALS CALLED DISPERSANTS CAN BE USED TO BREAK UP THE OIL. THEY WORK JUST LIKE DISH-WASHING DETERGENT AT HOME.
"UNFORTUNATELY, DISPERSANTS LEAVE BEHIND TOXIC MATTER FROM THE OIL THAT MAY STILL HARM HUMANS AND ANIMALS."

HIGH-PRESSURE HOSES ARE USED TO SPRAY HOT WATER AND CHEMICALS ON THE SHORELINE.
BUT, EVEN IF THEY CLEAN UP THE OIL, THESE CHEMICALS CAN SOMETIMES HAVE HARMFUL EFFECTS ON THE SURROUNDING ENVIRONMENT.

IT SOUNDS LIKE THERE'S NO EASY WAY TO CLEAN UP AN OIL SPILL.
THAT'S TRUE. BUT SCIENTISTS CONTINUE TO SEARCH FOR NEW WAYS TO SAFELY DEAL WITH OIL SPILLS.

"SCIENTISTS ARE LOOKING AT WAYS OF USING BACTERIA, OR TINY, ONE-CELLED CREATURES, AS A WAY OF CLEANING UP OIL SPILLS.
"THIS BACTERIA WOULD EAT THE CRUDE OIL.

"ALL LIVING THINGS NEED FOOD TO LIVE.
"BUT, DIFFERENT KINDS OF LIVING THINGS EAT DIFFERENT KINDS OF FOOD.

"FOR EXAMPLE, PLANTS USE SUNLIGHT TO PROCESS WATER AND CARBON DIOXIDE INTO FOOD.*
"COWS EAT GRASS AND OTHER PLANTS, AND HUMANS EAT BOTH THE MEAT FROM COWS AND THE PLANTS.
*THIS PROCESS IS CALLED PHOTOSYNTHESIS.

"SCIENTISTS HAVE DISCOVERED THAT SEVERAL SPECIES OF BACTERIA EAT CRUDE OIL, WHICH CAN BE TOXIC TO OTHER LIVING THINGS.
"USING BACTERIA OR PLANTS TO REMOVE POLLUTION FROM THE SOIL OR WATER IS CALLED BIOREMEDIATION."

OF COURSE, EVEN THOSE BACTERIA ARE NOT 100 PERCENT EFFECTIVE.
THE BEST WAY TO MAKE SURE THAT OIL SPILLS DON'T HARM THE ENVIRONMENT IS TO DO OUR BEST TO PREVENT SPILLS FROM HAPPENING IN THE FIRST PLACE.

"BY TAKING MASS TRANSIT, LIKE BUSES, OR RIDING BICYCLES, WE CAN REDUCE THE AMOUNT OF CRUDE OIL NEEDED FOR GASOLINE.
"RECYCLING CERTAIN KINDS OF PLASTIC WILL ALSO REDUCE OUR NEED FOR CRUDE OIL AS WELL AS THE AMOUNT OF OIL SHIPPED.

"YOU CAN ALSO WRITE TO GOVERNMENT OFFICIALS, ASKING THEM TO PASS LAWS THAT WILL MAKE THE OIL INDUSTRY SAFER.
"THE OIL POLLUTION ACT OF 1990 WAS PASSED AFTER THE EXXON VALDEZ SPILL. THIS LAW STATES THAT ALL U.S. TANKERS MUST BE BUILT STRONGER BY 2015.
"THE LAW ALSO STATES THAT OWNERS OF OIL TANKERS MUST HAVE A CLEANUP PLAN IN CASE OF AN OIL SPILL."

HUNDREDS OF INDIVIDUALS, INCLUDING MEMBERS OF GOVERNMENT AGENCIES AND VOLUNTEERS RESPONDED TO THE ATHOS 1 SPILL IN THE DELAWARE RIVER.
CLEANUP CREWS REMOVED OILY SOLIDS, LIKE DRIFTWOOD AND PLANTS.
VOLUNTEERS, LIKE MR. CLAUSEN AND HIS GROUP, HAND WASHED OIL-COVERED ROCKS.

OTHERS USED DISH-WASHING DETERGENT TO CLEAN THE OIL FROM WATERFOWL, LIKE CANADA GEESE, AND OTHER ANIMALS THAT LIVE ALONG THE SHORE OF THE RIVER.

THE U.S. COAST GUARD HAS REPORTED THAT THE ATHOS 1 HAD SPILLED ALMOST 300,000 GALLONS (1,135,623 L) OF OIL INTO THE DELAWARE RIVER. THIS WAS 10 TIMES MORE THAN ORIGINALLY GUESSED.
THE SPILL AFFECTED AROUND 115 MILES (185 KM) OF THE SHORELINE, KILLING OVER 200 BIRDS AND ANIMALS.
THE EFFORTS OF OFFICIAL AND VOLUNTEER CLEANUP CREWS PREVENTED THE SPILL FROM BEING FAR WORSE.
THE END.

Facts About Oil Spills

1. The United States uses about 700 million gallons (3 billion l) of oil every day.
2. The largest spill in the United States so far was the *Exxon Valdez* spill in 1989, which spilled almost 11 million gallons (42 million l) of crude oil.
3. The *Exxon Valdez* spill is only the thirty-fourth largest worldwide.
4. Scientists guess that only 5 percent of the oil that spills into the ocean comes from major oil spills.
5. About 33 percent enters the water in small amounts from people's activities.
6. More than 60 percent of oil that enters the water comes from natural seeps, or places in the ocean bottom where oil leaks out.
7. Just 1 quart (1 l) of oil can cause an oil slick almost 2 acres (1 ha) in size.
8. Offshore drilling can cause blowouts, when oil or gas gushes constantly from the well into the water. The biggest blowout lasted for nine months off the Mexico coast.
9. Oil pipelines often leak for a long time before people realize there is an opening in the pipe.
10. An oil spill does not have to be large to damage wildlife. In 1976, a small spill in the Baltic Sea killed more than 60,000 ducks.

GLOSSARY

BILLIONS (BIL-yunz) Thousands of millions. One billion is 1,000 millions.

CONTAINED (kun-TAYND) Held in.

DAMAGE (DA-mij) Harm.

DERRICKS (DER-iks) Towers over deep drill holes, such as oil wells.

DETERGENT (dih-TER-jent) A cleaner.

DISPERSED (dih-SPERSD) Broken up or spread out.

ENVIRONMENT (en-VY-ern-ment) All the living things and conditions of a place.

FOSSILIZED (FAH-suh-lyzd) Became the hardened remains of a dead animal or plant.

IMPACT (IM-pakt) An effect on someone or something.

RESERVOIRS (REH-zuh-vworz) Stored bodies of water.

SKIM (SKIM) To remove something from the surface, or top, of a liquid, such as water.

SPECIES (SPEE-sheez) A single kind of living thing. All people are one species.

TOXIC (TOK-sik) Poisonous, or harmful to plants or animals.

VOLUNTEERS (vah-lun-TEERZ) People who offer to work for no money.

INDEX

WEB SITES

Due to the changing nature of Internet links, PowerKids Press has developed an online list of Web sites related to the subject of this book. This site is updated regularly. Please use this link to access the list:

www.powerkidslinks.com/ged/sludge/